**A practical guide for leaders
at all levels who are
searching for significance!**

THE INSPIRATIONAL
LEADER

MICHEAL J. BURT

The Inspirational Leader
Copyright © 2005

ISBN: 1-59872-154-2

Layout and design: Mitzi T. Brandon

Editorial Assistance: Barbara Collie Floyd and Mitzi T. Brandon

First Printing: September 2005

Printed in the United States of America by InstantPublisher.com

For more information, visit:
www.maximumsuccess.org

Maximum Success
Speaking to, consulting, and working with organizations to create an environment of enthusiasm and action toward significance.

The Journey Continues

After writing my first book *Changing Lives Through Coaching* (geared primarily toward coaches) I sensed that it was time to do a spin-off that focused primarily on one of my real passions—leadership. Traveling the country as an inspirational speaker and author I have found that virtually everywhere people are fighting the same battles—developing the leadership skills and personal motivation needed to connect the dots between their thoughts and actions, being the person they really want to be, and having the lives they really want to have. Seldom through all my travels have I found a person who didn't know what type of leader he or she wanted to be, only to allow others, circumstances, or environmental factors push them into being a leader that they would seldom follow themselves. I have certainly fallen into this category over my leadership career many times. Developing the self-discipline, the only lasting form of discipline, to be the person at the end of the day that we set out to be in the morning should be our ultimate goal. When we develop that synergy between our talk and our walk then we're on our way to being happy, satisfied, and fulfilled.

This book will assist you to find your voice so that you can help others find theirs. People, now more than ever, want to be inspired, motivated, validated, appreciated, led, and affirmed. They do not want to be controlled, coerced, manipulated, or lied to. We are living in a knowledge worker age where the job of the great leader is to tap into the enormous reservoir of talent and potential inside each constituent. Will this be easy? Absolutely not, but it certainly will be challenging and will help to separate the pretenders from the real leaders. People want to wake up in the morning and go to a job they love in an organization they admire and work with a leader they believe in. We now understand how we invest our time and who we invest it with determines our quality of life, and I don't know about you, but I'm on this ride to connect to others and do something significant with my time and talents. At the end of the day I'm guessing you are on board for similar reasons.

Our goal each day as leaders is to become a leader that others choose to follow vs. have to follow. Once we get there we will be well on our way to igniting the fire within others and on our way to living a life of deep meaning and significant contribution. Best of luck on this journey. Remember this ride will be filled with peaks and valleys and trial and error so don't become frustrated—only motivated. Promise yourself at the end of everyday that you can look in the mirror and be satisfied with the person you ended up being, the same one you decided to be when you woke up.

Micheal

Micheal J. Burt

About Micheal Burt

Micheal began leading others at the young age of 15 when asked by a former coach to help coach a junior pro basketball team. It was then that his passion for leading and connecting to others began. At the age of 18 he began coaching as a profession at his alma mater Woodbury Grammar School, while he attended Middle Tennessee State University. He led the Cubs to their first ever State Championship in 1994. He then went to Riverdale High School as the head freshman coach and assistant varsity coach. His teams went 41-10, and at the ripe age of 22, he was named the head women's basketball coach at Riverdale High, making him the youngest head coach in the state of Tennessee. He is currently in his seventh year and has produced the most wins in a six-year period in Riverdale history. In addition to being an international speaker, author, consultant, and trainer, he is also founder and president of Maximum Success. This company speaks to, consults, and works with individuals and organizations to create an environment of enthusiasm and action toward significance. Micheal holds Bachelor of Science and Master's of Education degrees from Middle Tennessee State University and is currently pursing a Doctorate of Management in Organizational Leadership. He resides in Murfreesboro, Tennessee.

Acknowledgments

This book is dedicated to my father James Burt.
Thank you for being such a big part of my life.

Also, this dedication is extended to all the many
wonderful players and assistant coaches I have
worked with over the years. You have influenced me
just as much as I hope I have influenced you.

Teddy Taylor. Thank you for standing firm
about who you are and what you believe in.
I noticed and took heed.

Daryl Deason. Thank you for kick starting
my speaking career over twelve years ago.

Mitzi T. Brandon, thank you for helping me and
Maximum Success grow and for putting
a professional image on all our ideas.

Go to www.maximumsuccess.org to see what
Maximum Success has to offer you

Call: 615.849.2099

E-mail: coachburt@comcast.net

THE INSPIRATIONAL LEADER

A Practical Guide to Becoming a Leader Others Choose to Follow

As luck or timing would have it, I began writing this book while vacationing on a beach in Panama City. Imagine that. If you read my first book *Changing Lives through Coaching*, you know I began writing that one while vacationing in Destin, Florida. You're probably wondering what kind of person goes on vacation to work, and that is a legitimate question. Please allow me to explain. I had wrapped up a three-day speaking trip that began in Columbus, Georgia, following the cancellation of two flights in Atlanta in which the airline couldn't get my luggage to me, so I had to speak all day in a pair of khaki shorts, a gap t-shirt, and a pair of adidas tennis shoes. No wait it gets better. After speaking in the casual attire I drove to Albany for speaking engagement number two and then on through Georgia en route to my final destination, Panama City. As luck would have it, I got a speeding ticket on the way. What a trip so far!

Whenever I get down people are always the ones that inspire me to get back up, and the group I had in Panama City did just that. They were wonderfully receptive and reciprocated the energy I so desperately tried to bring to the table. Today people are looking for inspiration, and incidentally, the word inspire means to breathe life into another. Now more than ever I believe people want so badly to be inspired, led, motivated, validated, affirmed, and appreciated. They want to do something big with their lives and sometimes just need others, especially leaders, to breathe some life into them. That's ultimately what this book is all about. How to become an inspirational leader who taps into the unlimited potential of others. Don't get me wrong, I can be negative at any time, but I have learned it seldom gets me or others anywhere. You can be realistic and driven and still remain inspirational, so in this book which is a direct spin off of my first one, I will outline ways to bring out the best in your constituents. Understand this is a process and in the end the process will be just as important as the product. So hold on tight and see the big picture.

Why the Inspirational Leader?

When I developed the concept for this program and book I wanted to help leaders do something significant with their time and talents and, more than anything, I wanted to help people just like me who had the energy and enthusiasm but just needed some guidance. Beginning my leadership career at the age of 15 in a youth basketball organization, I needed direction and guidance about where to channel my newly found passion and energy. That's really what this book and my program titled "The Inspirational Leader" is all about. Putting into print the ideas, experiences, successes, and failures in a practical guide for the leader while knowing that you truly can be a "Difference Maker" was the ultimate goal. Through my experiences I believe all leaders have good intentions and want to make a difference but sometimes a blueprint for success is needed. I hope this book will satisfy that want or need.

I've always wanted to write a book and have always believed my experiences at such an early age could be of value to some of those who followed. I, just like you, want to do a lot of things with my life but usually don't because of a couple of ill founded reasons: fear of failure or fear of embarrassment. Neither one, to my knowledge, has killed anyone, but both have kept a lot of qualified people from reaching their hopes and dreams, and that is a shame. As I travel the country helping individuals and organizations do something significant with their time and talents one common theme has occurred to me. People are just down and need to be picked up. They are tired of being manipulated and lied to, motivated through fear, and coerced into doing something. Many people are not doing what they are passionate about for a living and get up every morning to lead others when they can't even inspire themselves. Now that's a challenge. To lead others you're going to have to get yourself together first so let's take a look at where you might fall on my maturity continuum. Personal organization and direction always supersede interpersonal organization. If you don't like where you are on this continuum then don't worry you most certainly can do something about it.

Category 1 (Reactors) - You are a reactive person that responds after the fact to whatever life throws at you. You wake up in the morning with little or no direction and float through the galaxy dodging bullets and just trying to "survive." If you're in this category, leading a group of people will be very difficult. After all, how can you lead others when you can't inspire yourself? This book will help you gain direction and purpose in life and with your leadership responsibilities as you accept the challenge of being a mentor to others.

Category 2 (Strugglers) - You know what you want to do with your life, but you don't know how to achieve it. You are frustrated and intimidated and think success is out there, but only for the lucky and the strong, and you don't perceive yourself to be in either of those two categories. Remember this: ALL the successful people started somewhere and many of them from less than glamorous situations. If you don't believe me just watch the hundreds of episodes of "Behind the Music" or any other biographical show that outlines a success story from virtually nothing. Decide today that you are going to be one of those people and get started. Remaining paralyzed will not get you anywhere but right where you are. Einstein said, "The significant problems we face in the world cannot be solved at the same level of thinking we were at when we created them." To get us anywhere or to

The Inspirational Leader

move forward we are absolutely going to have to do more than we used to. Joe Calloway, author of *Becoming a Category of One* said, "If you've been successful, you've figured out what worked up until yesterday."

Category 3 (Thinkers) - You know what you want and how to get it, but you are caught in an activity trap—the business of life—and you just can't get started on those hopes and dreams. These are the someday people. Next year I'll improve or be the person or leader that I envision. I just can't right now because I am so busy. There are certainly no guarantees for tomorrow and the last time I checked, today is the most important day of your life. Leadership expert John C. Maxwell says, "Yesterday's a cancelled check, tomorrow's a promissory note, so today is the only day that really matters." The first step on the path to greatness is to overcome inertia or the resistance to act. You've got all the tools so go for it. My motto is "There's only one way in life to profit, and that's by taking a risk." Stick your neck out and remember, you'll miss 100% of the shots you don't take and 100% of the dreams you don't pursue. The biggest gap leaders face is the one between what they know they *should* do and what they do. To make advancements in life we have to *take* action vs. *talking about* taking action.

Category 4 (Quick fixers) - You know what you want, you know how to get it, and you go out into the real world to try it, but you fail for reasons in and out of your control. As a result you become cynical and pessimistic about the process and just stay right where you are. Your failure reaffirms that you knew you couldn't attain your goal and your shortcoming is only proof of your non-existence and shallow thinking. Folks, the going rate for any worthwhile win is ten setbacks. The tenth try might be the trick and all the others could be unanswered prayers. Only time will tell but you're sure to fail if you feel sorry for yourself or think that people always get it right the first time. I've been rejected for several jobs and several situations in my life and all of them have turned out to be blessings in disguise. I'm sure you have your own list of what seemed to be a disaster at the time, only later to find out that what happened was one of the best things that ever happened to you. If you do fail a number of times, get in line with the millions of people that do so every day. Learn from it and move on to the next available opportunity. The right fit will certainly come along sooner rather than later if you focus on your circle of influence and keep improving your skills. Good things happen to people who keep on keeping on, learning from their mistakes, and adding value to other's lives.

Category 5 (Doers and Achievers) - You are the movers and shakers of the world. The average person can't keep up with you because the word average does not fit into your language system. You will be disappointed occasionally to find out that some of the world just doesn't get you and can't figure out why you just cannot be stagnant and quit trying to improve everything. The truth is that most of those people want to be like you and can't stand that you are making things happen. Expect a lot of resistance from many of the people you come in contact

The Inspirational Leader

with that absolutely are scared to death of change and live by this mentality. These people that try to keep you down believe that there is only one pie and if you are getting a bigger piece than them of whatever you are getting then there will not be enough left over. This mindset couldn't be further from the truth. There is enough out there for you and them to have as much as you would possibly like and are willing to get of whatever it is that you want—love, peace of mind, money, and happiness, etc. The abundance mentality teaches me to be happy for others' success and not jealous. You keep on keeping on, fight the good fight everyday, and know that you are doing something that matters and are proceeding in an upward spiral of improvement towards your hopes and dreams. Zig Ziglar said, "If you help enough people get what they want in their lives, you'll get what you want." I couldn't agree more. The level 5 people, or what Jim Collins referred to in "Good to Great" have a paradoxial blend of personal humility and professional will and are almost fanatically driven to take an organization and themselves to the next level. He stated that they are more "show horse" than "plow horse." Think about the best leaders you know and describe the qualities and attributes they have in your head. Isn't that really the type of leader you aspire to be. I would guess that you do have those talents just waiting to come out. Go on and let them out vs. suppressing them and you're well on your way to creating that synergy between "talk and walk" that I mentioned earlier.

Learning from the Knock Downs of Life

Remember this, adversity makes you stronger and many times frustration will eventually lead to action. One of my good friends and one heck of a basketball coach, Kyle Turnham once told me. "Frustration is just misguided enthusiasm." Boy was he right. People get frustrated because they want something on the inside to come out or they are hurting or disappointed and don't know how to express it. Understand that frustration and enough of it will eventually lead to action, and that is a good thing. God knows that when you fail it brings you closer to your creator. If not, he would have kept Joseph from going to jail, Jeremiah from falling into the slimy pit, Daniel out of the lion's den, and Paul from wrecking that ship three times, but he didn't. See adversity in your leadership and in your life as an inevitable part of the process of stepping stones to success versus stumbling blocks toward failure.

Reality Check:

When your intention to learn from your mistakes overcomes your fear of failure, that is when you are headed in the right direction.

Successful people turn thoughts into action. They close the execution gap that others only talk about.

ACT NOW!

PARADIGM SHIFTING:
THE COST OF CHANGE

C hange is a funny thing. I would guess that people in your part of the country do not like to change any more than they do in Murfreesboro, Tennessee, where I live. If you are trying to change from being negative to positive, from being dictator-like to practicing autonomy, or if you are trying to get people that you lead to change there are some obvious things you need to understand. First, you need to understand that satisfied needs do not motivate people, only unsatisfied needs do. So if you have a worker who comes to work for you everyday and doesn't want to be there, doesn't like the working environment, and doesn't like the people he or she works with then chances are you'll be getting the same pitiful performance as always. Why? Because you have allowed the behavior to continue, and there's no incentive or pain to change. Your employee is comfortable, and her needs are met. If you want her to change you must first understand this basic formula that a great mentor, Bill McEwen, once outlined for me:

Change=
F(pain, potential, practicality) >
The Cost of Change

Basically, Bill is suggesting that people change because of enough pain or enough potential in their lives, and I totally agree. Think about your personal or professional life when you changed something and I dare say it was because you were either sick and tired of being sick and tired or you saw some potential for yourself. Both of those things have to be practical and must outweigh the cost of change or you would probably have stayed right where you are and did what most Americans do—talk about changing. When it comes to you changing the way you lead people you must first break with the old thought and action patterns that are deeply embedded in you and move into a new style of leadership that is more in tune with your authentic self. Thomas Kuhn once stated, "Every significant breakthrough that we've experienced was first a break with an old thought pattern into a new way of thinking." This will be very difficult as those thought patterns and paradigms are most likely deeply embedded in you and will take some serious effort to change. When Apollo 11 first went to the moon it had no problem once it got out of the force field of the gravity of earth. Because of the gravity the most difficult part was the takeoff because the gravity was so hard to break through. Many times when you are trying to change something in your life such as your leadership style it is the first part of breaking old habits that is the hardest. Once you get past that part, it will be smooth sailing. Just like breaking an old habit and

The Inspirational Leader

beginning a new one, persistence, patience, passion, and perseverance will factor in.

Why Are You Leading?

My assumption is this: You are in a leadership position because you enjoy challenges or leading, want to move up the professional ladder, have been in a leadership position, or because someone somewhere saw the potential in you and believed you could coordinate tasks and efforts toward a common vision. I got started many years ago because others like Teddy Taylor, Daryl Deason, and Micki Vinson saw some potential in me and began to place me in leadership positions. Most of my leadership roles came through sports because of the communication and interpersonal skills, organization, and teamwork involved to be successful. In high school I was introduced to a number of clubs including an honor society called the Beta Club where I went on to be a national officer and was first introduced to public speaking. I did not know then as I went to different conventions speaking that ten years later I would be doing the exact same thing, just in bigger venues and to more people. It was really there that I began to grow as a leader and effective communicator to others. If someone asks you to be a leader it's because they see something in you that can be of value to other people, especially people who need guidance. Consider it a compliment and jump at the opportunity to expand your circle of influence. I don't know any other way to be part of a solution versus part of a challenge other than rolling my sleeves up and getting involved. That's one of the many things that my wonderful mother has taught me along this journey of life.

If you have chosen to do this, remember you now hold a tremendous responsibility to those under your guidance and leadership. You have expanded your influence greatly so promise yourself and your followers that you will do something significant with this golden opportunity. Life is about starts and stops. Between that time when you were born and the time you die is a space, or what motivational speaker Carol Anderson calls a dash on your tombstone. It's what you do with that space or dash in between the beginning and the ending that makes your life significant or insignificant, empty or fulfilled, a success or a failure. With this opportunity to lead, you have opened another chapter of your life and have a chance to do something that matters in that space. Make sure you make it count.

Just by purchasing this book you've indicated you want to improve and be a "difference maker." This is a practical, applied guide and you will learn about the process of succeeding and failing. I learned all about the process of education while pursuing both my Master's degree in Education and my Doctorate of Management in Organizational Leadership. There will be great moments of exhilarating learning coupled with awful moments of lonely despair when you just want to throw your hands up and move on. While in Atlanta in the summer of 2004 completing a residency for my doctorate degree, I literally wanted to quit and just come home. After much thought and soul searching, I knew I would enjoy the benefits immensely by continuing my education. I made it through by posting notes all over my hotel room that said Dr.

Micheal Burt on them. Sounds kind of catchy, don't you think? When you think about giving up, think of the benefits you will enjoy and see that light at the end of the tunnel. I promise it's not a train coming at you! Leadership will be exactly the same way, good moments and bad moments, but trust me the good will far outweigh the bad in the grand scheme of things.

This is by no means going to teach you how to lead in every situation or to solve all the complexities you will encounter. It will however serve as a resource to help eliminate some of the learning curve and heartaches that come with this challenging profession. If implemented correctly it will serve as a blueprint and a map to help navigate you through uncertain waters. Presented are principles I have used and methods and strategies which have been successful. I do believe they can offer some solutions to the complex problems you will encounter and through adequate preparation will steer you toward a level of success and significance. You decide what that level will be. I believe your fun meter should be on high everyday you work and live. We'll talk about the stages of life later, but for this to work you have to find the passion and infuse all you associate with it daily. This journey is going to be one you will never forget. Enjoy the ride, laugh at yourself some, and by all means remember those "little moments" (from the Brad Paisley song) because in the end they'll matter more than anything else.

You Better Find the Passion

As I work with people all across the country it still baffles me about the number of individuals who wake up every morning and go to a job they absolutely cannot stand. Many of us will be remembered by the legacies we leave in our careers and most people will work between 35-45 years of their lives. Maybe I'm different but I think you should absolutely love what you do for a living because I am convinced that is the only way that you will give your whole self to a cause. When you deem a cause not worthy of your most precious commodity—your time— then you will only give a part and receive a part in return. Passion is an irresistible motive for belief or action. It's what starts your engine, the reason you wake up in the morning, and is what gets you excited about pouring your heart and soul into something you believe in. To me, life is dull and mundane without passion. I know many speakers believe that this word is overused, but I'll have to respectfully disagree here. I want people working with me who are stark-raving maniacs about the projects we involve ourselves in because I want to be the best in the business wherever I decide to invest my time. I would argue that you didn't wake up this morning and say, "You know, I think I'm just going to survive today, just make it through the day. I want to be dead last or somewhere in the middle of my field." If those were your comments then there's little chance this book or anything else will help you become the leader you aspire to be. Success and leadership will be inconvenient many times as one of my good friends and Middle Tennessee Women's Basketball Coach Rick Insell always says. One day I was talking with my team about only giving a part of themselves to a cause so I began writing on the board how everything was interrelated and when I was done I thought, Wow! That

The Inspirational Leader

really made sense, and I basically summed up most of my philosophy on life in one step. It looked something like this. Try and put the pieces together and then I'll explain afterward. Now let me explain if you are completely lost. Your life is made up of time that we can't speed up, slow down, or stop for any reason. Having said that we can only determine our quality of life, not our quantity of life. How

---

Life
Time

Stimulus——Response	Habits
Self-Discipline	Intersection of Knowledge, Skill, and Desire
Self-Awareness	
Imagination	21-28 Days
Conscience	Value
Independent Will	Quality of Life
Choices	
Maturity	
Actions	
Consequences	
Continuum	

---

you invest your time (and who you invest it with) is a very important bet you make with your most prized commodity everyday. So, time is the most important thing we'll ever have. Each day we have thousands of stimuli and we respond based on what we value, the self-discipline we have, and the choices we make. Many times in between a stimulus (a thought we have) and the actual physical response we choose there is a space. In that space lies our freedom and ability to choose our response to virtually every situation we'll ever encounter. Because we have four unique human endowments, endowments that animals do not possess, we can utilize our self-awareness to know and identify what we need to improve, our imagination to create a better life for ourselves in our heads, our conscience, if properly educated to tell us right from wrong, and our independent will to act on our thoughts to create the life we really want versus the one we have. When we act on those thoughts a series of things happen because life is ultimately about three things: choices, actions, and consequences (both good and bad). If we act enough to build the proactive muscles in our hearts and minds we build habits (usually between 21-28 days) that become models for operating. When we decide what we value and have high levels of maturity we know what we want in life, what type of person or leader we want to be, and we act on those things because we have built the self-discipline to be that person. I illustrate this point primarily because saying what type of leader you want to be is vitally important, but of little value if you can't or won't do it consistently because of a breakdown in any of the above components. Simply put, when you're

The Inspirational Leader

passionate about something you value it enough and have the self-discipline to give your best during this process. If you're not, you will break down somewhere in between. Your job as a leader should be the intersection of where the needs of the world and your talents intersect, and I wouldn't have it any other way. For a deeper look at finding your passion and doing something significant with your life, look for my upcoming book *This Ain't No Practice Life* or go to www.maximumsuccess.org to order one.

One of my favorite authors Jim Collins outlined something similar in his book *Good to Great* when he introduced the Hedgehog concept within three semi-circles. He said to ask these three questions when going from good to great.

1. What are you passionate about?
2. What can you be the best in the world at doing?
3. What drives your economic engine?

His premise is that you can never be great at something unless you are passionate about it, can be the best in the world at it, or it satisfies your economic needs. Where your talent and the needs of the world intersect, therein lies your profession. When you can enjoy your work that much then you will have the enthusiasm and energy to lead others and your natural optimism will rub off on your constituents. Never underestimate the power of passion when it comes to the leadership of others. Again, this concept goes back to my idea that others want to be inspired, motivated, affirmed, validated, and appreciated. You can't provide that for others until you find your voice in life. Albert Schweitzer once said it best,

"In everyone's life, at some time, our inner fire goes out. It is then burst into flame by an encounter with another human being. We should all be thankful for those people who rekindle the inner spirit."

Why Understanding Others Will Help You Lead Them: Paradigm Trading

What is a paradigm and how do you shift it? A paradigm is the individual lens or mental map through which you see the world based on your scripting, molding, and experiences. It has also been defined as a set of assumptions, values, or practices for a community of people that share them. It has been developed throughout your entire life and is constantly being altered by your experiences. This fundamental understanding is central to your very thinking and from it will flow every thought, bias, perception, prejudice, and assumption you make. That in turn will affect how you make decisions, view this opportunity, and handle the many situations you will encounter while leading others. See it as a mental map from which you see the world. Please understand that the difference in your paradigm and others will cause you the most anxiety along this ride.

To lead a group of people you must get yourself in a mental place to make the difficult decisions you have to everyday in every situation. In one episode of my favorite TV drama "The West Wing," the chief of staff Leo McGherry informs the President of the United States, Jed Bartlett, that he must get himself into the right state of mind to order fighter missiles into war if necessary. The President notes that sometimes he must make decisions as the office of the Presidency separate from the man, Jed Bartlett. It's an important distinction. You should be completely authentic in your leadership but some decisions will be from "the leader." No, you won't be ordering any fighter jets into war although sometimes it will seem like some will be aimed at you. This is simply an illustration of you detaching yourself from your current state of being as a person into your role as a leader.

You must put aside your natural feelings and think about the betterment of the organization when making all decisions. You may not like some of the decisions you have to make, but after careful consideration and counsel from your staff you may have to make them. In reflection some of them will be wrong, but that is part of this process. All you can do then is go to any wronged party and offer a sincere apology. You would expect the same from your people. The people who are undisciplined or lack the intrinsic motivation to value their jobs or themselves may need to be monitored more than high-initiative-level people until they build the self-discipline to do the job at the level hoped for. With these people you may have to operate from a "tough love" paradigm. Trust me, 90 percent of them will thank you later and the other 10 percent will always blame you along with a host of other people for their failures in life. All you can do is your best based on the knowledge and information you have at the time of the decision. Live it, learn from it, and move on to the next challenge.

A big key that I believe in wholeheartedly from Collins' philosophy is getting the right people on the bus and the wrong people off. When you have the right people on board with you, chances are that you will see things from a similar paradigm philosophically. These people will seldom have to be motivated but rather placed in deep passion zones and empowered. The wrong people on the bus will simply suck the everliving energy out of you and the entire organization and will become a cancer that deteriorates other departments in your organization. Either get people on the bus that want to be there or get rid of them, it's just that simple.

Paradigm Shifting

When you change roles in your life, you experience a shift in your thinking. I experienced a huge one when I went from being an assistant coach to the head coach. Suddenly, I understood so many things I never did as an assistant. It happened when I changed titles and I certainly had an even deeper respect for the man who recommended me for my head coaching job, a great mentor and leader named Keith Short. Common paradigm shifts occur when you go from being single to married, not having children to having them, or change to a new job or place to live. Sometimes the way you see the problem is the problem and everything can be traced back to your paradigm, your way of thinking. To change something, you must first change the way you see it. This one concept will come in extremely handy when trying to understand your constituents and other situations you will encounter in this business. Everyone is getting pulled in some direction and based on their paradigms it may be increasingly difficult to understand them. Trying to practice empathic listening and working to see things from their perspective will help you better understand what buttons to push with them. I call this "paradigm trading." This where you place yourself in their shoes and they place themselves in yours. If you can't understand why they think the way they do, it will be extremely difficult to motivate them no matter what methodology you use. You must "get in their world." I'll admit some of the people I've led seemed to be on another planet. If that's the case, put your space suit on and get ready for the ride, it's bound to be an interesting one. Remember that the gaps in your paradigm and in the people you lead will present the biggest challenges in your leadership career. You should always search for respect vs. likeability as you move along because liking others revolves around moods, feelings, and utility power. Respect runs much deeper and will always last longer.

Growing Your Influence

Imagine that your influence begins with your own power of influence with yourself which involves you making and keeping commitments to yourself first before anyone else. As you begin to make and keep commitments to yourself and with the private victories needed to be consistent, you begin to slowly expand your influence with others as you walk your talk, deposit trust into others' emotional bank accounts, and be the person you say you want to be. Each step of the way your circle grows and expands with one person at a time until you have the power to influence others. This is called your circle of influence. Please remember this, your circle always begins with the inside/out approach and focuses on you first before others. Every time you create an advocate in another person you expand your circle of influence, and leadership is about influence, nothing more, nothing less.

I believe approach is everything in anything you do. No matter what level you lead, you must treat it like it's the biggest job and the most important thing you've ever done. Everyone will notice, and once you make it important, so will everyone else. If you are an up-and-coming leader remember this, "Everyday at your current job is an interview for your next job." I read Richard Carlson's book *Don't Sweat the Small Stuff* about not taking everything so seriously. When I finished I immediately threw it in the dumpster. I think if you want to be the best at anything you must sweat the small stuff and do what nobody else is willing to at any level. Leadership and success will most always be inconvenient, but when you pick up one end of the stick you pick up the other end as well. If you're not willing to sacrifice some things in your life then don't sign up to lead others. I think it is important to note here that you will be disappointed occasionally along this leadership ride, but the good moments will far make up for the bad, and when you see that light come on in another, you'll remember exactly why you are doing this. At the end of my first year of leading others probably the smartest thing I did was write a personal note to each one of my constituents. That was the beginning for me building an overriding purpose for an organization and caring about the people as people. I still to this day take time to write and e-mail people past, present, and future. If you take the time to write someone, even if it's just a short note, people know you care and they don't care how much you know until they know how much you care. Write those people today that have meant something to your life. This process is extremely gratifying and allows you to truly thank the people that have helped you to become the winner that you are today. Those people were "difference makers" in your life, and you should carry on that tradition in others.

Listed below are some strategies and thoughts for treating your current job as a stepping stone to the future successes in your life.

1. Remember this job is one of many steps along the journey of who you really want to be.
2. Focus on your individual improvement daily. Daily improvement helps you to transcend any marketplace and to see this job as fulfilling a much bigger mission in life than just picking up a pay check.
3. Leave a legacy. This is your real chance as most of us will be remembered by the legacies we leave in our jobs.
4. Tap the latent, undeveloped potential that is in each of us. At our deepest core we want to be a part of something bigger and try to expand our current boundaries in all dimensions. See your career as an opportunity to stretch who you are into the person you aspire to be.
5. See the big picture as this job relates to your quality of life. As mentioned earlier, how you invest your time and who you invest it with will directly affect your

quality of life. When you fully understand and comprehend that you are investing your most precious commodity—your time—at your workplace then you begin to see this as about connecting and helping others, and at the end of the week that's what we are all searching for.

6. Be mission driven. Wake up in the morning with a burning desire to be passionate about something, excel at it, and make money doing it. I really do believe if you chase being great at something then money will chase you all the way to the bank.

Are you walking your talk?

Great leaders develop a synergy between their walk and their talk!

The Inspirational Leader

CREATING A VISION:
WHY ON EARTH AM I HERE?

You have just expanded your circle of influence, now what are you going to do with that circle? Something that matters I hope. I joke with one of my best friends and a progressive sales rep with Murfreesboro Sporting Goods, Kim Rosamond, about how "today matters." Just to remind myself daily that slogan is written as my banner on my cell phone. Helping you reach your potential and doing something significant with your life is what this is all about and connecting to other people will always be the central theme of that concept. You must decide what this experience is going to consist of and develop guiding principles and models to draw from in times of adversity or question. If you want this to be more than just a job where others reach a financial end then you must create a plan and follow that plan daily to ensure you get the desired results you want out of the experience. Translating your mission to the moment will be the most difficult thing you will do in leading. My goal is to operate from a principle-center when running our organization. In the heat of the moment with pressure cooking, it's awfully easy to throw those principles out the window. This is where extreme self-discipline comes in. Think about the great mentors that you've had and remember how they conducted themselves in their moments. I would hope that they were steady and consistent and fully understood that with leadership there are going to be challenges along the ride. You have to know where you stand when it comes to your belief system. This will be very handy in the tough moments of your leadership career. Pat Riles once said, "You just gotta plant your feet and make a stand about who you are and what you believe in." Many times you can learn what to do and what not to do from other leaders in your field, and that will help you to decide your philosophy. Examine your motives, create a big picture, live from that picture in the good and bad moments, create a positive culture for growth and trust, and think about which category you are in right now in your leadership career:

Reactor - Reacts to everything and has no plan for movement or purpose

Struggler- Stays frustrated or intimidated by the marketplace

Thinker - Someday people that only think and talk about improving

Quick-fixer - Goes into the world and fails so becomes cynical about the process; sticks where they are and does not improve

Doer and Achiever - Movers and shakers of the world; level five people who act on their thoughts vs. converses about them; usually climbs to the top of the professional ladder quickly

The Inspirational Leader

As a leader you can make this process transactional, where your people come to work and there is little or no human investment made or potential tapped into, or you can make it transformational, where potential is met, talent is harnessed, and dreams are made realities. Which one sounds better to you? This is simple. The best leaders make this a transformational process and are true "difference makers" in the lives of their followers.

Now it is time to create that overriding purpose and to find a model for you. This might be the biggest decision you will ever make in leading others if you want this to be a life changing experience for you and the people under your guidance.

Building an Overriding Purpose for Your Organization–Vision

Most people have basic needs and have to choose how much of themselves they are going to commit to your cause. Stephen Covey contended in *The 8th Habit,* a book I highly recommend for the serious achiever, that there are four basic needs that humans have. The body has a need to live, the mind has a need to learn, the heart has a need to love, and the spirit has a need to leave a legacy. By tapping into these unique needs you can get more out of the people you are leading. On a commitment continuum Covey says there are different stages of commitment as represented in the following descending order .

Level 6 - Creative Excitement

Level 5 - Heartfelt Commitment

Level 4 - Cheerful Cooperation

Level 3 - Willing Compliance

Level 2 - Malicious Obedience

Level 1 - Rebel or Quit

It is my guess that most leaders operate at the second and third level on this continuum and the best leaders strive daily to get to level four, five, or six with the best organizations in the world reaching creative excitement as consistently as possible.

Building a purpose for your organization is an absolute must. I'm confused that so few leaders verbalize what their purpose is. I think all leaders want to operate from a paradigm of integrity, trustworthiness, honesty, fairness, kindness, compassion, and sincerity, and they want their players to reciprocate that to them and each other. To develop constituents "holistically" from a mental, physical, emotional, and spiritual standpoint you must develop these dimensions daily not just every once in a while. Stephen Covey refers to the holistic model as the "whole person theory." To expect a follower to be honest while you allow dishonesty in the workplace is sending strong messages of duplicity and will cause chronic problems in your organization. I believe the way to do this is to create a nice balance between all dimensions and plan them as part of your daily interaction with your people. You have a tremendous opportunity to influence many people and you

The Inspirational Leader

must look for "teachable moments and meaningful conversations" to do just that. Teaching life skills as part of work always made sense to me. It is common sense but not always common practice that our jobs are all about adding value to other's lives and to the organizations to which we belong. Finding a model to do that from that was consistent and based on timeless principles that followers could benefit from in the long run, while also offering a structure for decision making made the most sense. In college I found my tool in the most profound book I ever read, Covey's *The 7 Habits of Highly Effective People*. These 7 habits offer a reference point for virtually all decisions you will encounter. I believe so much in these principles that one of my lifelong goals has been to work for the Franklin Covey company delivering seminars and training sessions on the 7 Habits to people and organizations across the country. I became a certified facilitator of "The 7 Habits" in 2004 and have been spreading the message ever since. In 2005 we will successfully implement this model with every freshman student who enters into Riverdale High School where I teach and coach. When a person enters our organization one thing is certain, they will be taught these 7 habits, and they will be reinforced throughout their tenure with us. My hope is that they become embedded into their value system and also become a reference point for their future decision making process.

The 7 Habits are:

Habit 1: Be Proactive

Habit 2: Begin with the End in Mind

Habit 3: Put First Things First

Habit 4: Think Win-Win

Habit 5: Seek first to Understand, Then to be Understood

Habit 6: Synergize

Habit 7: Sharpen the Saw

Note: *As I discussed earlier in the book, in 2004 Covey released his latest addition to the habits:*

Habit 8: Finding Your Voice and Helping Others Find Theirs

Throughout the course of this book you will see me refer to these habits again and again. They have had a profound impact on both my personal and professional life. I believe they will positively affect your life if you vigorously implement them into your value system and into the workplace.

Recently I have also immersed myself into studying Jim Collins' *Good to Great* book which also offers a valid and researched methodology for building an organization to last. I cannot stress enough the value in adopting habits of effective people and of effective organizations. It is my sincere belief that great leaders and great people who have the fortitude to make a series of good decisions build great organizations and attract the best people. As times and

The Inspirational Leader

society changes it is vitally important to have principles and habits that do not change. You develop a changeless core that does not change among the permanent whitewater that you will encounter in the marketplace.

Incorporating Life Strategies into your Philosophy as a Mentor, Guide, and Facilitator

John Maxwell says in *Today Matters* that your life is made in your daily agenda. I agree wholeheartedly. Everyday must be seen as an opportunity to teach and offer direction to your people. I have a sign outside my office above a special group of people that have come through my organization, and it says, "This organization builds advocates and lifelong memories." What does your organization build? What do we need most in the world to accomplish the big tasks we set out to accomplish? The help, talent, potential, and capital of others will be the only way to truly reach for the stars. Start today by implementing life strategies at work to help your people when they need you the most. It appears from my view point that we need people in the workplace that have the skill set, tool set, and mind set to go beyond current boundaries and to not just survive on a daily basis.

As I say this I want you to understand, you're not going to have meaningful conversations twelve hours per day with your people, but you can deposit positive statements and actions into their emotional bank accounts when you interact with them. One thing that greatly puzzles me is the lack of training and teaching of how to

The Inspirational Leader   37

successfully interact and express ourselves with others whether it is in the workplace or in a personal relationship. Teaching communication skills to all your people and effective ways to express them will be integral to being a great leader. People appreciate, although sometimes quietly, learning valuable lessons on something that is rarely ever taught, how to be successful in relationships. I still haven't figured out how our whole lives are built on our connections with other people but there are no classes taught during our primitive years on specific dynamics to improve those relationships. I guess that's for another book. This is just one example of how to incorporate an overriding purpose into your organization. Take any book or program that you think offers value to people's lives, especially to communication and building effective teams, and make it the topic of your staff meetings or interactions with your people. My rule is 50 percent on life and 50 percent on work.

Incorporating Life Strategies into the Workplace

1. Bring in experts or speakers on life topics about potential, building successful relationships, change, balance in life, goal setting, or personal motivation. (Book me today @ www.maximumsuccess.org, ha!)

2. Teach a series of lessons learned such as John Maxwell's "The 17 Indisputable Laws of Teamwork" or "The 21 Irrefutable Laws of Leadership, "The Fish Philosophy," "Who Moved My Cheese," "Good to Great," "The 7 Habits," "Principle-Centered Leadership."

3. Go to team building events or off site retreats such as ropes courses or Paintball (Maximum Success offers "The Ultimate Teambuilding Experience" as a nature retreat for organizations to build all the intangibles needed for significance. See www.maximumsuccess.org for more details.)

4. Spend 10 minutes each day with a different worker (I take a walk with my staff.) to just talk about their particular lives and what you can to do to help improve.

5. Increase the training in your organization to include mission building, relationship improvement in the workplace, diversity training, or time management skills and encourage workers to continue to "sharpen their saws" individually.

6. Have the workers lead certain meetings to put them in leadership positions and to experience paradigm shifting. (This is a form of cross training.)

The most important point in this is simple: create a purpose and vehicle in which you can teach life skills while working with others. I believe with my whole heart that all of us want to give a part of ourselves to everyone we come in contact with. Your career offers you the means to give away your gift. Please don't ever take that for granted. Develop your overriding purpose today. You'll find out in the next chapter that you'll have to make the most of your most precious commodity, your time. It's not slowing down for anyone and it plays no favorites. The million dollar question is what are you doing with yours?

Great leaders are also great followers!

It is time for you to become the leader you envision yourself to be!

MAXIMIZING YOUR TIME:
NOT ENOUGH HOURS IN THE WEEK, WHAT WILL I DO?

I think every person should wake up in the morning with a purpose and a reason for living. If you have been selected or have been chosen to be a leader then you already have one—you have to help people go from where they are to where they need to go. You've also got to help people tap into the enormous human capital and potential that they have. I think that is a pretty big reason to wake up in the morning. As I outlined earlier, your life is made up of a limited amount of time. How you choose to spend it will certainly determine your quality of life, so in this section I want to open your eyes to how most people spend theirs. What if I told you that the average person spends 23 years sleeping, 9 ½ years in the car, 6 years eating, 1 year in religious activity, 6 months to a year at red lights, 140 days making and unmaking the bed, between 15-20 years in some form of education, and the real kicker, between 35-45 years working. Now how important is your time? It is estimated that 70 percent of all people do not like their jobs, and the average person spends 12-14 hours per day working just to get through what is on their plates (let alone doing anything significant or important to them), and 88 percent say it is hard to balance personal and professional life. The average person receives six voice mail messages per day, sits in 1.6 meetings that 85 percent say are unimportant and 88 percent say had absolutely nothing to do with the mission of the organization. Now how important is your time? My point is this, there is no such thing as time management. At many of the seminars I teach across the country people want to know how they can better manage their time, and the point is that you can't. You don't manage time. You spend it with people you care about, you invest it in things and people you deem worthy, or you flat out waste it, it is that simple. The key to managing your time is to decide what is most important to you (quality of life) and place those things, those people, and those activities in your time. Many times the people I work with allow things, agendas, and work schedules to dominate their lives and take the approach of victim when that could not be further from the truth. You control your life and you certainly control how you invest your time. Don't ever let anyone else tell you any different.

Think about this. If I were to give you $86,400 per day and told you that at 12:00 a.m. you lost any you didn't use and it did not carry over until the next day, what would you do with that money? Typical answers I get at seminars are spend it, invest it, or waste it. Those are all good answers. You have something far more precious than $86,400 per day although that's hard to believe. You have 86,400 seconds per day, and you are probably falling into one of the three mentioned categories: you're either spending it, investing it, or flat out wasting it. Smart people try to spend and invest their 168 hours per week in activities and people that make them happy and fulfilled. It is also vitally important to have a nice balance between your personal and professional life. If you get all of your satisfaction off the job or on the job, then it is time to evaluate the quality of the things you are spending your time on in other areas.

Now that you have a better understanding of how people spend their time, you need to understand that everyday you make four bets with yours. Mark Leblanc, owner of Small Business Success, and the biggest person who influenced me to write my first book says that, "Everyday you make four bets: your time, energy, money, and creativity." I agree. What goes into your time here will ultimately come out on the other end. Be a poor planner and you'll get poor results and guess who everyone will blame for that performance, the leader.

There are two simple models you can use when it comes to your organization. Organize, act, and evaluate, and continue, stop, and start. These are simple concepts but will pay enormous dividends. Leading is a continual process of adjustment based on seeing the need and filling the need and something you must do daily. Always remember, "Where there's no gardener, there's no garden." Think about how much you're tending to your garden. As I discuss the importance of planning the use of your time it is vitally important to know and connect to your mission in life and to do that you need a mission statement or defining statement. Now if you have never dealt with mission statements don't be scared they don't have to get all mushy. This is simply a defining statement or constitution that offers guidance and support in living and fighting the daily battles you will encounter. If done properly, this document you come up with can be very powerful.

Formulating a Mission Statement

How important is a mission statement or what some people call a defining statement? It depends on how much you draw from it. If it is the constitution and you follow it and all decisions flow from that model, then it is very powerful. If it is merely a piece of paper placed somewhere to make it appear that you possess a mission then don't even bother putting one together. I am a big believer that you should live your life out of design not from default. If you let others dictate and decide what your life is going to mean, then chances are they will put you in a situation that is non-threatening to them, and guess who's losing, both of you. I do believe that your fun meter should be on high when you are working and living your life. When you're unhappy your constituents sense it and can tell you are not immersed in the moment. When debating over what your mission statement should say think of this. Write one sentence that describes you and what you have to offer. Then place the guiding principles of how you are going to get the desired results you want. For example, here is the defining statement for my company Maximum Success:

Maximum Success is a company that speaks to, consults, and works with organizations that want to create an environment of enthusiasm and action toward significance.

How do we do that?
Through our programs "How to Become the Inspirational Leader," "Developing the Winner Within," "The Leadership Academy," and "This Ain't No Practice Life."

From what principles do we operate?
"The 7 Habits of Highly Effective People" and Covey's 8th Habit.

In this example I show you what our defining statement is, how we get our desired results, and what principles are our guiding lights. I would be happy to help you develop a mission statement. For help just go to www.maximumsuccess.org.

Following is my personal and professional mission statement from which I strive to live from daily. Notice at the top it has four powerful words that my good friend Bill McEwen also includes in his mission statement. I too, agree that these four things are needed to be successful in today's society.

PASSION
PERSISTENCE   PATIENCE   PERSEVERANCE

To live fully,

To influence many,

To learn daily,

To love without judgment,

To leave a legacy for those that follow,

To think big,

To act on those thoughts,

To help others detect their passion and reach their potential,

To model maturity and wisdom,

To forgive those who have transgressed against me,

To be a "difference maker,"

To sacrifice for the greater good,

To continue to seek guidance and spirituality,

And to live a life that matters.

Live like I was dying.

Just this past year I added the popular Tim McGraw song "Live Like You Were Dying" to the bottom of my mission statement because I believe it is the ultimate mission statement. Just think if you were to live like you were dying. Every person that had ever transgressed against you, you would forgive because you know that life is just too short for you to hold that bitter pill deep inside. Every person that you had transgressed against you would call and ask for their forgiveness because you wouldn't believe in making enemies, only advocates. Every person that you needed to spend time with or pick up the phone and call to tell that you love then you would and wouldn't make any excuse not to. You would literally "live like you were dying." A great friend of mine, Stacie Childress, an excellent thinker and basketball coach sent me an e-mail once that said, "Treat every person that you come in contact with today as if they were going to die by midnight tonight." Think about if you carried this philosophy with you to work every day. And since we're on models to live by I want to share with you one that Covey outlined in *The 8th Habit* that I think is very much on target.

Four Assumptions to Live by Daily

1. *For the body*—assume you have had a heart attack; now live accordingly.
2. *For the mind*—assume the half-life of your profession is two years; now prepare accordingly.
3. *For the heart*—assume everything you say about another, they can overhear; now speak accordingly.
4. *For the spirit*—assume you have a one-on-one meeting with your creator once a quarter; now live accordingly.

These assumptions are powerful and worth noting and living by because they put us in touch with our authentic self and the person we really want to become. Now having outlined some examples of mission statements it is important to have this with you as you plan your weekly engagements because this helps you to create balance and is a constant reminder of what is deeply important to you. Many studies indicate that only one-half of all people are satisfied with the work they have done at the end of the week. Do you fall into that category? If you do I submit that it is because you are not doing what you are passionate about for a living or you are living a life that is not in congruence with what really matters most to you.

Success is all in the eyes of the beholder and is constantly being redefined.

The Time Matrix and Beginning This Process

The most informative book I've read on producing the best use of time is Stephen Covey's *First Things First*. In the book he shows you the traditional time management paradigms and introduces you to a fourth generation matrix that focuses on quality of life, re-creation, reconnection, building relationships, and overall planning. The context of this is simple. If you have a certain amount of time allotted while living your life and leading your group you must carefully and skillfully plan the high value activities that will go into that time. Here are some important tips for maximizing your time and for doing what is deeply important to you therefore producing quality of life results.

1. Create a mission statement or defining statement for how you want to live your life. Remember you write the book of your life, and you live the book. It would also be helpful to write a mission statement for how you will handle your business at work.
2. Make a weekly plan based on your master plan's objectives. Plan your week on Sunday during quiet, uninterrupted time and place.
3. Outline your roles for the week and do not exceed seven (7). Roles could include leader, husband, wife, son, daughter, friend, homeowner, etc. I think it is vitally important that one of the roles just be you.
4. Outline one or two goals for each role that you want to improve on this week.
5. Outline these four dimensions and outline one goal this week for each dimension (this offers balance):
   a. Physical—Exercise 4-6x
   b. Mental—Finish book *Good to Great*
   c. Social/Emotional—Have fun/mend relationships
   d. Spiritual—Connect to who I am/me time
6. Once you have outlined these things, begin to place the tasks you have in your calendar during the week and assign As, Bs, and Cs to them with A being highest priority, B being things that can get pushed to the next day and C being things you only do when you feel inspired. This helps you to prioritize the most important things in your week.

7. Translate your mission to the moments in your daily agenda based on what is deeply important to you.
8. Complete three high-value activities (activities that yield the most results when time is invested) per day toward your goals from the master plan (laser-like focus) (again from Mark Leblanc).
9. Reset your counter each week. This will help you to develop a laser-like focus and singleness of purpose toward your goals.
10. If your entire planning system consists of post-it notes located everywhere, run to the store and get a new planning system immediately. (I strongly recommend the Franklin Covey Planning System and reading the book *First Things First* by Stephen Covey.)

This planning system offers you the opportunity to invest your time in areas that mean the most to you, therefore producing a higher quality of life result. As a leader it is important where you are going to spend your time and world. Below are a list of things on which most of the leaders I know focus their time.

- Leading
- Vision creation
- Building better teams
- Motivating others
- Delegating
- Empowering
- Creating synergy or collaboration
- Building relationships
- Executing
- Solving problems

The Inspirational Leader

Now take a few moments and circle the things that you really want to be great at, not just good and visualize ways that you can invest your time there to make it happen. My three biggest rocks when investing my time are creating a vision, building relationships with my people, and executing the ideas we have.

Achieving Balance

A hot topic across the country right now is achieving balance and how to accomplish it. If truth be told, most successful people I know seem off balance as they are driven by the need to succeed and to leave a legacy in their organization. Make no mistake about it, inspirational leaders are driven to succeed but not just in one role of their lives, all roles. Granted, you will not be great at everything and a laser-like focus and singleness of purpose will be needed to achieve anything significant or worth having. Simply put, success in one role does not justify failure in another. Here are some simple strategies that I recommend for achieving that ever elusive balance in your life:

1. Leave your work at work and your home at home. Don't clutter up the other by bringing crossover to the table.
2. Find stress relievers and comfort zones for relaxing.
3. Find a hobby that you absolutely love and can immerse yourself in.
4. Take mini vacations.
5. Seek spiritual balance and know what you stand for.

6. Exercise regularly.
7. Get involved with a cause you deem worthy outside of work.
8. Take time for renewal in these four areas: physical, mental, social/emotional, and spiritual.

Take time for the little pleasures in life and work to create balance in all four of your dimensions.

Where Are We and Where do We Want to Go–Pathfinding

The first step is to evaluate your constituents from a mental and physical standpoint and make an assessment of the skill level and psychological level. Making the mistake of operating at a higher level than what your followers can function at is counterproductive to your cause. It does not matter how much knowledge you have. You must be able to translate and relate it to your people wherever they are in their lives. I equate this to an example of calling a dog. If you stand and call the dog it might come to you five out of ten times. If you get on the floor (the dog's level) it will almost inevitably come to you every time. You must get on their level, whatever that is. If you are leading whipper snappers right out of high school, then the chances are pretty strong that they see things differently than you do. If for one second you think that your paradigm and theirs is the same then that is your management problem, not theirs. A hard day's work for you might be coming in at 6 a.m., working through lunch, and taking it to the house around 6 p.m. A hard day's work for them may be coming in at 10 a.m., working till noon, taking a two- hour lunch, coming back at 2:00, and leaving at 4:00 (while trying to keep their pants up because of the apparent shortage of belts in today's society). My point here is common sense, but seldom common practice. You truly have to meet your people wherever they are in their lives, whether it be younger or much older, and try to take them to the next level. I am asked many times by younger managers the best ways to manage or lead people that are much older or have been in the company a lot longer than them. My first advice would be for you to try to get them to believe that you are working with them and that they are not working for you, but with you. Finding what they really enjoy (passion) and outlining their strength zones will be vitally important to the success of this relationship.

Execution and Focus

The biggest problem both at the personal level and at the professional level that I see people struggle with is the execution gap between saying something and doing something. It is virtually everywhere and certainly universal. Daily execution is vitally important to your success. View it as though you are the architect of your new house. Your blueprint will be the end product of that design. Every day you plan your work you are building the success or failure of that house. Through successful repetition followers will know how to handle situations. That successful repetition comes through proper training and execution. As leaders, many times we become upset with our people only to reflect that we have done a poor job of preparing them for those situations beforehand. When planning your day there are some important things to consider:

1. What are the big rocks to include today?
2. How much time do you want to devote to a certain activity?
3. Everything should be built on cooperation and only competition vs. one's self not teammates.
4. How does this tie in to our overall mission?
5. Whom can I help today to be successful?
6. How can I add value to someone's life today?
7. How can I work toward leaving the legacy in my department and with my organization?
8. Teach, teach, and re-teach and coach your people all the time.

Once you have led for a while you will have a strong sense of what you stand for from a philosophical standpoint, and this process will become increasingly easier. Never underestimate the power of practice; it truly is the foundation for your success or lack thereof.

What Are People Looking for from YOU–the Leader?

Think about yourself for a second and think about the ideal leaders in your life, the ones that you openly chose to follow vs. had to follow. Those people probably saw the potential in you, the good when it was easy to see the bad. They validated your feelings, affirmed your worth, appreciated your efforts, picked you up when you were down, wouldn't allow you to quit when you wanted to, and motivated you to be your best. When your experience with them was over, perhaps you looked back immediately or after years and thought, "That person helped to make me into the person I am today, and without them there would have been no success."

The same thing you are looking for in others is what they are looking for in you. The best definition of leadership in my opinion is defined in Covey's *8th Habit* as communicating to people their worth and potential so clearly that they come to see it in themselves. Isn't that what all leaders are trying to do? Communicate to their constituents their own value so they come to believe it themselves? Others are looking for you to lead them through inspiration and enthusiasm and your belief in them and the mission that you deem worthy together. If you could follow you then chances are they could to. Be a leader that you could follow on a daily basis.

Being a "Difference Maker" and Building Lifelong Relationships

When is the last time you came in contact with someone in your life and after experiencing something with them you decided that they were a "difference maker"? I've had many people walk in and out of my life, each leaving a piece of them with me, and they truly were "difference makers." There were too many to mention but their belief in me reaffirmed who I was and encouraged me to find my true voice in life. Throughout my educational journey many teachers and professors have changed the way I think, respond to situations, and approach leadership. The point is this: For the people under your guidance you need to be a "difference maker," and change their lives, help change their paradigm, and be a constant source of guidance of strength and wisdom among the trials and tribulations of life. To do this you must make the most important investment ever, and that is a human investment. Talk, communicate, or just sit quietly with the people in your organization. Remember the important moments of their lives. Be there when they need you the most and always make them feel special. This journey will not always be an easy one. The breaking down of bad habits and the reforming of new ones will be a difficult process, but if they respect you they will run through the wall for you. Likewise, you must do the same for them. The leadership process is the beginning of what could and should become a lifelong relationship. I know many leaders that when their guidance ends they move on to their current or future workers and forget about the past. Remember this, those people of the past helped to pave the way for the present and future. It was through their blood, sweat, tears, and sacrifice to a cause bigger than themselves that you have what you have today. Do not forget that legacy, and certainly do not let your employees forget it. Here are some easy ways to build relationships that will last.

1. Go out of your way to let them know you are non-judgmental and will always be there for them.
2. Write personal letters at significant moments of their lives.
3. Focus on the positive in they are going through difficult times.
4. Go for a walk and just talk about life or take them to lunch.
5. Be understanding when the situation arises.
6. Look for moments to highlight their achievements and contributions to the team.
7. Plan times to have deep, meaningful conversations about life and their current roles at work.
8. Learn what makes them tick, what motivates or pushes them away, and act accordingly.
9. Always remember, they are human just like you.
10. Plan events for reunions after the experience and keep in touch.
11. Always invite them back to work with you (keep it in the family).

These are just a few of the ways to develop a lifelong relationship. I realize that they are just traveling through your life and you through theirs, for only a moment in time; however, if approached correctly that moment may be the best one of their lives. Tie your overriding purpose to the daily agenda and sit back and watch fireworks happen as your relationship grows. Your goal: When it is all said and done you want your people to say, my leader was a "difference maker." I'll take that compliment any day, won't you?

Your goal:

**For your people to say,
"My leader was a
difference maker."**

The Inspirational Leader

BEGINNING WITH THE END IN MIND:
YOUR ORGANIZATION

All things are created twice, first mentally and then physically. Question: Why don't people live out those beautiful pictures they paint in their minds about what they want to do with their lives? The last time I checked you have only one life on this earth, right? My answer: Fear of failure or fear of embarrassment or they just don't want to put that much work into it. The law of the harvest says that you reap what you sow and sooner or later everything that goes around comes around. Think about that the next time you're investing in something. This section is about painting a picture in your mind about how you want your group to look like in the end and living from that picture daily. Here's an interesting story to help illustrate my point. When I was completing my first residency for my doctorate it was so taxing mentally that I really wondered if I could make it through it but I asked myself this question, "If I do make it then what will I do with that degree, what doors will open, and how will I make a significant contribution to society?" Those were all questions that others and I asked. At the end of the residency my professors, Dr. Mike Vandermark and Dr. Richard Klein, both psychologists, had us complete an exercise. We were to go into the year 2012, five years after we had completed our doctorate degree, and let the class know what our lives were like and how we were using our degrees. The neat part was that we got to introduce ourselves as Dr. The point here is self-evident. We were painting that picture of what we would be doing in the future. To get there we must sacrifice daily to enjoy the benefits in the long run. Life is funny, usually what you put in, you get back. Have you ever seen anyone only put in 25 cents and get a dollar soda out of the machine? I use that illustration with my team all the time. Another example would be for you to place yourself mentally at your own funeral personally or at your own leadership funeral. Bear with me on this one, I know it's tough. What would your eulogy say? If you want that eulogy to say that you were kind, compassionate, empathetic, trusting, loyal, inspirational, or any other adjective to describe you then you must translate that mission to the moment when living everyday. I want mine to say, "He was a 'difference maker' in the lives of millions." Your work should be the exact same way. You must paint a picture of what competencies and characteristics you want your team members to display and act from that paradigm daily. I want my constituents after working for me to be positive, contributing, responsible, and enthusiastic members of society. For them to get there, we must practice those qualities each and every day. Research tells us that you can learn or unlearn any habit in 21-28 days. You have more than 21 to teach your people the qualities you think are

The Inspirational Leader

critical to success. One of your major responsibilities is to teach and model behavior qualities of a person that is searching for significance and guide them to the promised land.

Success is all in the eye of the beholder and is constantly being redefined. If you set certain goals and your timeframe does not match those goals, go back to the drawing board and redefine them. As I mentioned earlier, you should reset your goals every 30 days or so and evaluate where you are and where you want to go. I've always been in awe of entertainers and musicians, but I have stuck to what I know best and that is leading people. Find your passion point and reach for the stars! I promise you that your people will feed off your enthusiasm. Redefine what success is and search for significance, doing something bigger, than just picking up a paycheck. Be a transition person that takes potential and turns it into reality for those taking the journey with you. What's a reasonable benchmark for this group? The next section will help with that elusive question. Remember this, once you've reached a certain plateau of success it will be easy to become complacent, but inspirational people only look to go to the next level and you should too.

Creating Reasonable Benchmarks

When it is all said and done each person you deal with wants one thing, a positive experience and to know that they invested their time in a cause they deemed worthy. They want to know you treated them with respect, believed in them as a human being, and brought out the best in them. They may disagree from time to time with the methods you chose to use, but they can at least respect that you gave it your best shot. Goals, I believe, are the most over said and underdone thing in the world today. Do they have tremendous value? Yes, but too many people say they want one thing and act the total opposite when trying to attain it. For this to be of value to you and your followers you must determine your definition of success. Is profit the bottom line? Is it the improvement of every person in your organization? Is it maximizing everyone's potential as much as possible? Is it overachieving? I believe success is a tricky term, because one person's success may mean failure to another. I believe wholeheartedly in the word significance. For me, teaching each follower life skills, the 7 Habits, time management, resilience, teamwork, self-discipline, and belief in each other and the system is significant. I believe getting up every morning and trying to influence people in a positive way and improving both their character and competence while teaching them things they need to make it in life is success. For me, it is that simple. If you don't have any personal benchmarks for your life, I would encourage you to get some now. They give you direction and something to always reach for, and overreaching is a positive action for anybody. If you have low-initiative-level people under your guidance create daily benchmarks for them each day and hold them accountable for those assignments. High initiative people will be able to just go and do and report back to you, but others may need a push in the right direction.

Potential and What Is It?

Potential is the idea of embryonic growth from the time you are born until the time you die. There is virtually no way to measure it and no way to measure whether your people have it or not. Make up your mind what success is and don't let anyone talk you out of it. You may have to redefine it as you go if you don't reach the benchmarks you set forth, but that's no excuse not to pursue them.

Dealing with People and Meeting Challenges Together

Dealing with people is the tough part of leading. Negative people alone have driven a lot of great leaders out of this profession. Unrealistic expectations, lack of basic knowledge of the situation, difference in paradigms, and emotionality are all challenges when dealing with others. Leaders approach work from a team standpoint and understand that teams are made up only of a group of individuals. If the individual brings flaws to the table then they become group flaws. People (or most of them) focus solely on what is in their best interests, promoting themselves at the expense of the group. Our society has become so caught up in the social mirror that we feel embarrassed if we do not succeed or make mistakes while trying, so we search for excuses or someone to blame and many times that person is the leader. First of all people must understand one thing, self-confidence is not given or taken away from anyone unless they choose to give it away. Not even the most powerful leader can destroy someone's confidence if it has been deeply embedded in them from their primitive years, it's just that simple. I hear the old cliché so many times that a person has taken another person's confidence from them. This is possibly only if the person didn't have confidence to begin. The confident people in the world take everything in stride and did not waiver much regardless of how critical I was of them. This is a power or powerless concept. Habit 1 of "The 7 Habits" that we teach is "Be Proactive" and at its basic root shows that we are all ultimately responsible for the success or failure of our lives. We are able to respond to do what we need to. Teaching this concept as a leader is vitally important. Poor leadership will limit a person's ability and degrading comments certainly will not work. Teaching others that their success lies between their stimulus and response is imperative to this process.

Understand up front that you and some of your followers will probably never see things from the same perspective. Accept it and don't take it personally. I have seen some of the most vindictive things done by people all in the sake of vanity and protecting their own interests. When emotionality factors in, rationality goes out the window. Below is a list of recommendations to facilitate some level of success in this relationship:

1. Search for respect vs. likeability.
2. Focus on steadiness throughout the relationship as there will be peaks and valleys.
3. Clarify your expectations up front with an introductory session and formal training.
4. Keep the relationship professional and be wary of crossing that line.

The Inspirational Leader

5. Keep your personal life separate from your professional life.
6. Think "what if" when you make decisions.
7. Keep people informed (Web sites, newsletters, e-mail list, etc.).
8. Never, never, never meet with a person when emotions are high.
9. Always keep your composure.
10. Set a meeting time up to 3-5 days later after an incident if a person wants a meeting (cool down theory).

These are just some of the suggestions I have after leading others for the last thirteen years. If you have a specific question then e-mail me at coachburt@ comcast.net and I will be glad to help you through your dilemma or offer my advice. The fact is that you really must all be on the same page for the process to fully reach its maximum level. If your people are not sold on you or your initiatives, a negative undercurrent of resistance will be created and will result in a vicious cycle of disrespect and underachievement. I just wish more people understood that this cycle is totally counter-productive to what everyone really wants, which is tapping into the full capacity of each person. We have tried to facilitate the gap that exists by creating the program "The Inspirational Leader" and "The Leadership Academy" and taking these programs across the United States to improve these relationships. Improving this gap is one of my ultimate goals in life. Best of luck as you are sure to run into many challenges with people throughout your leadership career and don't ever get out of leading by letting someone else define who you are or what you stand for. When you decide to get out then do it because you sincerely think you have lost your effectiveness, not because you are running from unpleasant environmental factors.

Surrounding Yourself with Quality People and Acquiring a Staff

Putting together a quality team of your own when it comes to your staff is so important. You simply can't do everything and catch everything by yourself no matter what level you are leading. The success of your group or organization rises and falls with the leadership. I've been fortunate to have some great assistant coaches, including one of my truly best friends Barry Messer. He is to this day the most loyal assistant I have ever had. Other great assistants included Tara Solomon James, Kathy Dye, Kelly Chastain, and Jessica Jackson. My current staff is infused with a true winner and team player in Wendi Scott (a future leader of her own organization), and a truly great young woman named Regan Vaughn. When hiring a staff it is important to do a thorough background search to find out the whole story to the person. Why do they want to leave where they are, how do they interact with others, what are their work levels, can you trust them, are you compatible with them, and their motives are just some of the questions to answer. I search for people who want to move up the leadership ladder and who are not satisfied with being followers. People who want to move up are hungry and will do what it takes to help the organization. Compatibility is critical in these situations. Having too many Type A personalities on staff or too many passive personalities could be a recipe for disaster. My personality is strong so I search for people to complement that. If you can only settle for one or two characteristics in people or your pool of candidates is limited then the trump card is loyalty and character. If you can only get a warm body, then search for loyalty. You can teach them everything else. Character and competence is hard to find especially if you don't have much to offer. What I have found in leadership is that if you can sell them on yourself and your vision then they probably will come on board because they too believe in the greater good. Those people are diamonds in the rough. Wendi Scott is one of those people. She has the character and competence to be a "difference maker" and she certainly will in her lifetime. When hiring others throw out the term essential job functions and put in the term preferred job functions. Jim Collins in his book *Good to Great* wrote, "We expected good-to-great leaders would begin by setting a new vision and strategy. We found instead that they first got the right people on the bus, the wrong people off the bus, and the right people in the right seats—and then they figured out where to drive it." After all my travels across the United States and trying to figure out the keys to successful organizations, it appears that the biggest factor is finding the right people and getting rid of the wrong people. I would assume that there are people in your organization that need to get off the bus and be replaced with some who need to be on board. Find the winners and hire them, and your job will be so much easier.

Purpose Driven Leadership— What Is It Really About?

I am convinced that Rick Warren's book *The Purpose-Driven Life* is so popular because so many people are searching for what they need to be doing with their lives. It is my belief that everyone wants to contribute significantly to the world by detecting and fulfilling their passion and helping others find theirs. That inner voice that inspires you to greatness is uniquely yours, and although untapped many times, does continue to exist. I got into leadership first to win in sports, but quickly realized it was about so much more. It has evolved into leading, influencing, and searching for the moments of significance that I will always treasure. Motivating someone to find their inner voice, standing on principles, and leaving a legacy for others to follow now precede the superficial reasons for being a leader. It's funny how that happens. Now, building a vision, believing in each other, doing the right thing, and making a difference are the real reasons I lead others. It's about purpose and meaning. Profiting and winning is just a bi-product of getting people to believe in themselves first and each other second, and boy that is fun. I enjoy speaking, consulting, and connecting with others but deep in my veins and at my center I love leading others, and I suspect you will too. This has got to be about more than just making money or picking up a paycheck. It's got to be about life and all of its joy and sorrow. Gordon B. Hinckley, at age 92 said it best,

I am no longer a young man filled with energy and vitality. I'm given to meditation and prayer. I would enjoy sitting in a rocker, swallowing prescriptions, listening to soft music, and contemplating the things of the universe. But such activity offers no challenge and makes no contribution. I wish to be up and doing. I wish to use every waking hour to give encouragement, to bless those whose burdens are heavy, to build faith and strength of testimony. It is the presence of wonderful people which stimulates the adrenaline. It is the look of love in their eyes which gives me energy.

Leadership is about using our time and energy wisely and moving to an age of wisdom when leading others. It's about a mission to connect and help others overreach and find their true calling in life and get as close as possible to reaching their hidden potential. Now, that's a whole lot bigger reason for waking up in the morning then just managing or supervising others. I wake up with a purpose to improve my organization and enrich the lives of those I lead, it's just that simple. Why do you wake up?

Develop Self Discipline

**Developing the self-discipline,
the only lasting form of discipline,
to be the person at the end of the day
that we set out to be in the morning
should be our ultimate goal.**

The Inspirational Leader

GOING OUT A WINNER:
TO LIVE, TO LEARN, TO LOVE, TO LEAVE A LEGACY

With each speaking engagement I accept and each year I spend leading others, I evolve into the leader I personally aspire to be. I can honestly say that I am just now tipping the iceberg of being the leader I sought out to become over thirteen years ago. I assume your journey will be the exact same way. Every day leaders wake up all across the country and fight the same battles of uneven levels of commitment, lack of motivation in the workplace, hidden agendas, and selfish motives, but each day there is a follower who wakes up and wants so badly to be inspired and motivated. Those are the people that you wake up to lead. Along this journey I have found the neatest of discoveries, and that is the discovery of self and my passion area of developing leaders in others. I suspect if you dig down deep in your heart that you will reconnect or find yours. Life sometimes falls into predictable stages of passion, duty, burden, and then commitment. Always remember that to do something significant with your life that you must always reconnect with the passion because it is there that the seeds of greatness exist just waiting to blossom. Many people look at life and see only the negative as if it were a mission impossible. I look at life and say why not? Decide today that you are going to be a leader that others openly choose to follow, not one they have to follow. The people you lead are just humans like you, and they hold unlimited potential. Possibly you are the person that can unlock those gates. If you will develop that potential and push them to new limits, then they will be forever grateful to you and you to them. My motto has always been "To live, to learn, to love, and to leave a legacy." Decide what type of leader you aspire to be and set out each morning to be that person and promise yourself each night that you were. The hardest thing you'll ever have to do will be to create that synergy between your walk and talk. Go out a winner in all you do because "This Ain't No Practice Life." Thank you so much for taking this journey with me, but more importantly for stepping up to the plate and accepting "The Leadership Challenge." Now go make those hopes and dreams a reality! God bless you and each one of the people that you lead.

Micheal

Program Information

Micheal conducts his flagship programs The Leadership Academy, This Ain't No Practice Life, and The Inspirational Leader across the United States. He works with organizations, colleges, and companies to create an environment of enthusiasm and action toward significance. Micheal is a certified facilitator of Stephen Covey's "7 Habits of Highly Effective People" within his organization and has inspired thousands over his career. He is also a trainer and consultant for SkillPath leading seminars and on-site consulting across the country on "Excelling as a First time Manager or Supervisor"

Depending on your format, time availability, and meeting objectives, his presentations can run from 50 minutes to a three-day retreat. Allow Micheal to truly take you and your people to the next level with one of his inspirational programs. His energy and enthusiasm will awake the winner within each of you.

Contact Maximum Success today to take you and your people to the next level. Programs offered by Maximum Success:

This Ain't No Practice Life

The Leadership Academy

The Inspirational Leader

Developing the Winner Within

The Ultimate Team Building Experience

Creating Stark Raving Fans through Unbelievable Customer Service

For booking information contact,
Maximum Success
615.849.2099
or go to www.maximumsuccess.org

Buy Micheal's first book
Changing Lives through Coaching
at www.maximumsuccess.org

Look for Micheal's next book
This Ain't No Practice Life
due out soon

Bibliography Page:

Collins, J. (2001). *Good to Great*. New York: Harper Collins.

Covey, S. (1989). *The 7 Habits of Highly Effective People*. New York: Fireside.

Covey, S. (2004). *The 8th Habit*. New York: Fireside.

LeBlanc, M. (2003). *Growing Your Business*. MN: Expert Publishing.

Maxwell, J. (2004). T*oday Matters*. New York: Time Warner.

Kouzes, J. & Posner, B. (2002). T*he Leadership Challenge*. San Francisco: John Wiley & Sons.

Warner, Rick. (2002). *The Purpose-Driven Life*. Grand Rapids: Zondervan.

Ziglar, Z. (1997). *Over The Top*. New York: Thomas Nelson.

Comments

Micheal certainly brought out the "leaders within" at our annual managers retreat. Everyone who attended left feeling empowered to take this organization from "good to great." What an inspirational speaker Micheal is.

Nell Womack-Moore, Director of Human Resources
Murfreesboro Medical Clinic and SurgiCenter

Micheal Burt is a visionary who has a firm grasp on promoting positive change. Every young person who has the pleasure of working with Micheal will become a better person. As a parent, I am grateful for leaders such as Micheal, because he truly cares for young people.

Bill Spurlock, Assistant Principal, Riverdale High School

As you know, a pearl of great price is not worth the asking. From my vantage point, you got the pearl, the case, and the store! Keep winning.

Colby B. Jubenville, Ph.D., Associate Professor and Coordinator,
Sport Management, Middle Tennessee State University

You have found a great pearl if you are holding **The Inspirational Leader**. *Micheal Burt will take you from "good to great" if you will believe in the truth that he is offering.*

Tony Woodall, CEO, Southeast Team Sports

Micheal's presentation was electric. If you were not energized when you came out of this seminar, you don't have a heart beat. If you want your associates to work with you and not for you, I highly recommend Micheal Burt's Leadership Academy.

Marc Larson, General Manager, Crane Interiors, INC.